✕ SQA

2016 SQA Past Papers With Answers

National 5
SPANISH

FREE
audio files to accompany this title can be accessed at
www.hoddergibson.co.uk
• Click on the turquoise 'Updates and Extras' box.
• Look for the 'SQA Papers Audio Files' heading and click the 'Browse' button beneath.
• You will then find the files listed by language and level.

2014, 2015 & 2016 Exams

National 5 SPANISH

✕SQA

D1579742

HODDER GIBSON
AN HACHETTE UK COMPANY

This book contains the official SQA 2014, 2015 and 2016 Exams for National 5 Spanish, with associated SQA-approved answers modified from the official marking instructions that accompany the paper.

In addition the book contains study skills advice. This has been specially commissioned by Hodder Gibson, and has been written by experienced senior teachers and examiners in line with the new National 5 syllabus and assessment outlines. This is not SQA material but has been devised to provide further guidance for National 5 examinations.

Hodder Gibson is grateful to the copyright holders, as credited on the final page of the Answer Section, for permission to use their material. Every effort has been made to trace the copyright holders and to obtain their permission for the use of copyright material. Hodder Gibson will be happy to receive information allowing us to rectify any error or omission in future editions.

Hachette UK's policy is to use papers that are natural, renewable and recyclable products and made from wood grown in sustainable forests. The logging and manufacturing processes are expected to conform to the environmental regulations of the country of origin.

Orders: please contact Bookpoint Ltd, 130 Park Drive, Milton Park, Abingdon, Oxon OX14 4SE. Telephone: (44) 01235 827720. Fax: (44) 01235 400454. Lines are open 9.00–5.00, Monday to Saturday, with a 24-hour message answering service. Visit our website at www.hoddereducation.co.uk. Hodder Gibson can be contacted direct on: Tel: 0141 333 4650; Fax: 0141 404 8188; email: hoddergibson@hodder.co.uk

This collection first published in 2016 by
Hodder Gibson, an imprint of Hodder Education,
An Hachette UK Company
211 St Vincent Street
Glasgow G2 5QY

Typeset by Aptara, Inc.

Printed in the UK

A catalogue record for this title is available from the British Library

ISBN: 978-1-4718-9121-2

3 2 1

2017 2016

Introduction

Study Skills – what you need to know to pass exams!

Pause for thought

Many students might skip quickly through a page like this. After all, we all know how to revise. Do you really though?

Think about this:

"IF YOU ALWAYS DO WHAT YOU ALWAYS DO, YOU WILL ALWAYS GET WHAT YOU HAVE ALWAYS GOT."

Do you like the grades you get? Do you want to do better? If you get full marks in your assessment, then that's great! Change nothing! This section is just to help you get that little bit better than you already are.

There are two main parts to the advice on offer here. The first part highlights fairly obvious things but which are also very important. The second part makes suggestions about revision that you might not have thought about but which WILL help you.

Part 1

DOH! It's so obvious but …

Start revising in good time

Don't leave it until the last minute – this will make you panic.

Make a revision timetable that sets out work time AND play time.

Sleep and eat!

Obvious really, and very helpful. Avoid arguments or stressful things too – even games that wind you up. You need to be fit, awake and focused!

Know your place!

Make sure you know exactly **WHEN and WHERE** your exams are.

Know your enemy!

Make sure you know what to expect in the exam.

How is the paper structured?

How much time is there for each question?

What types of question are involved?

Which topics seem to come up time and time again?

Which topics are your strongest and which are your weakest?

Are all topics compulsory or are there choices?

Learn by DOING!

There is no substitute for past papers and practice papers – they are simply essential! Tackling this collection of papers and answers is exactly the right thing to be doing as your exams approach.

Part 2

People learn in different ways. Some like low light, some bright. Some like early morning, some like evening / night. Some prefer warm, some prefer cold. But everyone uses their BRAIN and the brain works when it is active. Passive learning – sitting gazing at notes – is the most INEFFICIENT way to learn anything. Below you will find tips and ideas for making your revision more effective and maybe even more enjoyable. What follows gets your brain active, and active learning works!

Activity 1 – Stop and review

Step 1

When you have done no more than 5 minutes of revision reading STOP!

Step 2

Write a heading in your own words which sums up the topic you have been revising.

Step 3

Write a summary of what you have revised in no more than two sentences. Don't fool yourself by saying, "I know it, but I cannot put it into words". That just means you don't know it well enough. If you cannot write your summary, revise that section again, knowing that you must write a summary at the end of it. Many of you will have notebooks full of blue/black ink writing. Many of the pages will not be especially attractive or memorable so try to liven them up a bit with colour as you are reviewing and rewriting. **This is a great memory aid, and memory is the most important thing.**

Activity 2 – Use technology!

Why should everything be written down? Have you thought about "mental" maps, diagrams, cartoons and colour to help you learn? And rather than write down notes, why not record your revision material?

What about having a text message revision session with friends? Keep in touch with them to find out how and what they are revising and share ideas and questions.

Why not make a video diary where you tell the camera what you are doing, what you think you have learned and what you still have to do? No one has to see or hear it, but the process of having to organise your thoughts in a formal way to explain something is a very important learning practice.

Be sure to make use of electronic files. You could begin to summarise your class notes. Your typing might be slow, but it will get faster and the typed notes will be easier to read than the scribbles in your class notes. Try to add different fonts and colours to make your work stand out. You can easily Google relevant pictures, cartoons and diagrams which you can copy and paste to make your work more attractive and **MEMORABLE**.

Activity 3 – This is it. Do this and you will know lots!

Step 1

In this task you must be very honest with yourself! Find the SQA syllabus for your subject (www.sqa.org.uk). Look at how it is broken down into main topics called MANDATORY knowledge. That means stuff you MUST know.

Step 2

BEFORE you do ANY revision on this topic, write a list of everything that you already know about the subject. It might be quite a long list but you only need to write it once. It shows you all the information that is already in your long-term memory so you know what parts you do not need to revise!

Step 3

Pick a chapter or section from your book or revision notes. Choose a fairly large section or a whole chapter to get the most out of this activity.

With a buddy, use Skype, Facetime, Twitter or any other communication you have, to play the game "If this is the answer, what is the question?". For example, if you are revising Geography and the answer you provide is "meander", your buddy would have to make up a question like "What is the word that describes a feature of a river where it flows slowly and bends often from side to side?".

Make up 10 "answers" based on the content of the chapter or section you are using. Give this to your buddy to solve while you solve theirs.

Step 4

Construct a wordsearch of at least 10 × 10 squares. You can make it as big as you like but keep it realistic. Work together with a group of friends. Many apps allow you to make wordsearch puzzles online. The words and phrases can go in any direction and phrases can be split. Your puzzle must only contain facts linked to the topic you are revising. Your task is to find 10 bits of information to hide in your puzzle, but you must not repeat information that you used in Step 3. DO NOT show where the words are. Fill up empty squares with random letters. Remember to keep a note of where your answers are hidden but do not show your friends. When you have a complete puzzle, exchange it with a friend to solve each other's puzzle.

Step 5

Now make up 10 questions (not "answers" this time) based on the same chapter used in the previous two tasks. Again, you must find NEW information that you have not yet used. Now it's getting hard to find that new information! Again, give your questions to a friend to answer.

Step 6

As you have been doing the puzzles, your brain has been actively searching for new information. Now write a NEW LIST that contains only the new information you have discovered when doing the puzzles. Your new list is the one to look at repeatedly for short bursts over the next few days. Try to remember more and more of it without looking at it. After a few days, you should be able to add words from your second list to your first list as you increase the information in your long-term memory.

FINALLY! Be inspired...

Make a list of different revision ideas and beside each one write **THINGS I HAVE** tried, **THINGS I WILL** try and **THINGS I MIGHT** try. Don't be scared of trying something new.

And remember – "FAIL TO PREPARE AND PREPARE TO FAIL!"

National 5 Spanish

The course

The National 5 Spanish course aims to enable you to develop the ability to read, listen, talk and write in Spanish, that is to understand and use Spanish, and to apply your knowledge and understanding of the language. The course offers the opportunity to develop detailed language skills in the real-life contexts of society, learning, employability, and culture.

How the course is graded

The course assessment will take the form of a performance and a written exam.

- The performance will be a presentation and discussion with your teacher, which will be recorded and marked by your teacher.
- The written exam will take place in May and this book will help you practise for it.

The exams

Reading and Writing

- Exam time: 1 hour 30 minutes
- Total marks: 50
- Weighting in final grade: 50%

What you have to do

- Read three passages of just under 200 words each, and answer questions about them in English.
- Write 120–150 words in Spanish in the form of an email, applying for a job or work placement: there will be six bullet points for you to address.

Listening

- Exam time: 25 minutes
- Total marks: 20
- Weighting in final grade: 20%

What you have to do

- Part 1: listen to a presentation in Spanish, and answer questions in English.
- Part 2: listen to a conversation in Spanish, and answer questions about it in English.

How to improve your mark!

Every year, examiners notice the same kind of mistakes being made, and they also regularly come across some excellent work. They give advice in the three key areas of reading, listening and writing to help students do better. Here are some key points from their advice.

Reading

Make sure that your Reading answers include detail. Use each question as a guide to where to look, and what to look for. In the question there will be a clear guide to the context for the answer. Detailed answers are generally required, so pay particular attention to words like "más", "siempre", "bastante", etc. and to negatives. "Los sábados por la tarde" isn't just Saturday, and "a principios del mes de agosto" isn't just August, so be prepared to give all the details you can find.

Make sure you get the details of numbers, days, times etc. right.

Take care when using a dictionary when a word has more than one meaning. Learn to choose the correct meaning from a list of meanings in the dictionary.

Beware of false friends: "compartir" means share, not compare, and "esta de buen humor" does not mean he has a sense of humour, rather he is in a good mood.

In responding to the questions in the Reading papers, you should be guided by the number of points awarded for each question. You should give as much detail in your answer as you have understood, but you should not put down everything which is in the original text, as you would be wasting time. The question itself usually indicates the amount of information required by stating in bold, e.g. "**Mention 2 of them**". Often there are more than two possibilities, but choose the two you are happiest with and stick to them. Watch out for questions where two details are required for one mark. When you must give two details for the one mark, it will be highlighted in bold in the question.

Note that there will be a question in one of the reading papers which asks about the overall purpose of the writing. This will always be a "supported" question such as a box to tick or a true/false choice.

You should re-read your answers to make sure that they make sense and that your English expression is as good as it can be.

Listening

This is the paper that improves most with practice. So use the listening papers in this book several times to get used to the format of the exam.

Not giving enough detail is still a major reason for candidates losing marks. Many answers are correct as far as they go, but are not sufficiently detailed to score marks. The rules for Reading also apply here.

You hear each of the Listening texts three times, so make use of the third listening to check the accuracy and specific details of your answers.

Be sure you are able to give accurate answers through confident knowledge of numbers, common adjectives, weather expressions, prepositions and question words, so that some of the "easier" points of information are not lost through lack of sufficiently accurate details.

In responding to the questions in the Listening papers, you should be guided by the number of points awarded for each question, and by the wording of the question. You should give as much detail in your answer as you have understood, but you should not write down everything you hear. The question itself usually indicates the amount of information required by stating in bold, e.g. "**Mention 2 of them**".

Make sure you put a line through any notes you have made.

Writing

This, along with Talking, is often where students do best. However, frequently, the language used by candidates tackling Writing dips to a basic level and leads to pieces not being truly developed. Make sure you have some good material prepared and learned, ready to use in the exam.

Also, where learners write pieces that are too lengthy, this certainly does not help their performance. So stick to 20–30 words per bullet point.

On the whole, the majority of candidates write well, and the range of language used is impressive. So look at the success criteria in the answer section and try to model your Writing on it. This applies particularly to the last two bullet points.

You should ensure that you are careful when you read the information regarding the job you are applying for, and make sure your answer is tailored to fit that. Depending on the job, you may have to alter your strengths or the experience you are claiming. Use your dictionary to make sure you know what the job actually is, if necessary.

Use the dictionary to check the accuracy of what you have written (spelling, accents, genders etc.) but not to create new sentences, particularly when dealing with the last two bullet points. You should have everything you need prepared when you come into the exam.

Be aware of the extended criteria to be used in assessing performances in Writing, so that you know what is required in terms of content, accuracy, range and variety of language to achieve the "good" and "very good" categories. Ensure that your handwriting is legible (particularly when writing in Spanish) and distinguish clearly between rough notes and what you wish to be considered as final answers. Make sure you score out your notes!

You should bear the following points in mind:

- There are six bullet points to answer: the first four are always the same, the last two vary from year to year.
- Each of the first four bullet points should have between 20 and 30 words to address it properly.
- To get a mark of satisfactory or above, you must address the last two bullet points properly.
- You will need to have at least 15–20 words for each of these last two points, but do not try to write too much for these.
- You will be assessed on how well you have answered the points, and on the accuracy of your language.
- For a mark of "good" or "very good", you should have some complex language, such as longer, varied sentences and conjunctions.

Good luck!

Remember that the rewards for passing National 5 Spanish are well worth it! Your pass will help you get the future you want for yourself. In the exam, be confident in your own ability. If you're not sure how to answer a question, trust your instincts and give it a go anyway – keep calm and don't panic! GOOD LUCK!

NATIONAL 5

2014

National Qualifications 2014

X769/75/01

Mark

Spanish Reading

FRIDAY, 30 MAY

9:00 AM — 10:30 AM

Fill in these boxes and read what is printed below.

Full name of centre

Town

Forename(s)

Surname

Number of seat

Date of birth

Day   Month   Year

Scottish candidate number

Total marks — 30

Attempt ALL questions.

Write your answers clearly, in **English**, in the spaces provided in this booklet.

You may use a Spanish dictionary.

Additional space for answers is provided at the end of this booklet. If you use this space you must clearly identify the question number you are attempting.

Use **blue** or **black** ink.

There is a separate question and answer booklet for Writing. You must complete your answer for Writing in the question and answer booklet for Writing.

Before leaving the examination room you must give both booklets to the Invigilator; if you do not, you may lose all the marks for this paper.

Total marks — 30

Attempt ALL questions

Text 1

You read an article about Erasmus – a grant for European university students.

Para muchos estudiantes universitarios, recibir una beca Erasmus es la mejor manera de compaginar los estudios con el deseo de viajar y vivir en otro país europeo. Son miles los estudiantes europeos que se han aprovechado de esta beca popular.

Casilda Chico, 23 años

"El impacto del programa Erasmus supuso un cambio enorme en mi vida. Al llegar a Bruselas en Belgica, descubrí una ciudad nueva, diferente a la mía. Además, estar en Bruselas me permitió visitar los alrededores, empaparme de otra cultura y pasármelo muy bien!".

Angela Durán, 30 años

"Yo me fui a Londres, Inglaterra. Aprendí infinidad de cosas nuevas, pero lo que más me gustó fue que volví a casa sabiendo hablar inglés, supe adaptarme a otro sistema educativo que el español y a relacionarme con otra serie de personas. Fue una experiencia impagable".

Santiago Arroyo, 30 años

"Pasé mi año en Venecia en Italia. Recuerdo que ningún día era igual que el anterior y que siempre había algo que hacer. No hay mejor sensación que la de ser estudiante en el extranjero y de ser capaz de desenvolverse en una ciudad desconocida y en otro idioma. La experiencia SQA cambió mi manera de ver el mundo".

MARKS | DO NOT WRITE IN THIS MARGIN

Text 1 Questions

(a) For many university students, an Erasmus grant allows them to combine different things with studying. What are they?   **2**

_____

_____

(b) (i) For Casilda Chico, what was the impact of taking part in the Erasmus programme?   **1**

_____

(ii) According to Casilda, what were the advantages of studying in Brussels? State any **two** things.   **2**

_____

_____

(c) Give details of what Angela Durán liked most about her time spent studying in London. State any **two** things.   **2**

_____

_____

(d) (i) What does Santiago Arroyo remember about his year in Venice? State **two** things.   **2**

_____

_____

(ii) What did this experience change for him?   **1**

_____

_____

[Turn over

DO NOT
WRITE IN
THIS
MARGIN

Text 2

You read a web article about the Mexican actor, Gael García Bernal.

Gael García Bernal

Su carrera cinematográfica

El actor mexicano Gael García Bernal empezó su carrera artística actuando en el teatro y a la edad de once años actuó en su primera telenovela.

Desde entonces, Gael ha protagonizado las películas mexicanas más populares de los últimos tiempos y fue el protagonista de "Los diarios de motocicleta", película de gran éxito internacional que narró las aventuras de dos jóvenes argentinos que hacen un viaje en motocicleta por territorio suramericano. Su reciente película es una película política, pero también es graciosa y te emociona mucho.

Un gran activista social y político

Además, Gael es un gran activista social y político. Invierte mucho tiempo y energía en promover las campañas de Oxfam y en trabajar en defensa de la población más vulnerable.

Hace unos años, Gael visitó unas granjas en la región de Chiapas en México, donde descubrió lo difícil que era la vida para los granjeros. Ellos se quejan del sistema de comercio injusto.

La cumbre de las Naciones Unidas

Gael hizo un llamamiento a los líderes mundiales para combatir el cambio climático. Fue a la cumbre de las Naciones Unidas donde asistió a reuniones, discutió ideas, presentó estudios de casos, habló con los medios y entregó peticiones.

MARKS | DO NOT WRITE IN THIS MARGIN

Text 2 Questions

(a) How did Gael García Bernal's early career begin? State **two** things.   2

_____

_____

(b) The second paragraph tells us about two of his films.

   (i) How does the article describe Gael's film, "Los diarios de motocicleta"?   1

     _____

   (ii) How does the article describe Gael's **recent** film? State any **two** things.   2

     _____

     _____

(c) Gael is also a social and political activist. Complete the sentence.

He invests a lot of time and energy in _____

and in working for _____ .   2

(d) What did he find out when he visited Chiapas in Mexico?   1

_____

_____

(e) Gael went to the United Nations summit on climate change. What did he do there? State any **two** things.   2

_____

_____

[Turn over

Text 3

You read an article about job companies in Spain.

Las habilidades y competencias más buscadas por las empresas españolas

En el mundo laboral, existen ciertas habilidades y competencias importantes.

La informática

Tener conocimiento de las redes sociales es algo casi imprescindible en ámbitos como la publicidad, los negocios o la comunicación. Las empresas han prestado más atención a las redes sociales con el objetivo de lograr una buena reputación corporativa y para establecer contactos comerciales. Casi todas las profesiones tienen al menos un pequeño componente tecnológico y por eso, los empleados deberían saber utilizar bases de datos y buscar información por Internet.

Los idiomas

Las nuevas tecnologías han potenciado la importancia de más de una lengua. En España, el inglés se pone cada vez más útil porque gran parte de las aplicaciones y programas que utilizamos están en inglés.

Trabajadores proactivos

Las empresas valoran trabajadores con la capacidad de hacer frente a los problemas del día a día, con el deseo de comenzar nuevos proyectos y la habilidad de solucionar dificultades imprevistas.

El trabajo en equipo

Hoy en día las empresas están formadas por grandes equipos y los empleados tienen que trabajar juntos diariamente. Por lo tanto la capacidad de entenderse con los colegas es importante.

MARKS

Text 3 Questions

(a) According to the article, knowledge of social networks is extremely important in many areas. Name any **two** areas.　　　2

_____

_____

(b) What are the aims of companies that use social networks?　　　2

_____

_____

(c) What should most employees be able to do? Complete the sentence.

Most employees should be able to _____

and _____.　　　2

(d) The article goes on to talk about the importance of languages. Why is English becoming more useful in the world of work?　　　1

_____

(e) What do companies value in their employees? State any **two** things.　　　2

_____

_____

(f) In your opinion, what is the purpose of the article? Tick (✓) the correct box.　　　1

It gives you advice on how to find a job.	
It gives you advice on what skills you need in a job.	
It gives you advice on the best jobs to do.	

[END OF QUESTION PAPER]

ADDITIONAL SPACE FOR ANSWERS

ADDITIONAL SPACE FOR ANSWERS

[BLANK PAGE]

DO NOT WRITE ON THIS PAGE

Mark

N5

National
Qualifications
2014

X769/75/02

Spanish Writing

FRIDAY, 30 MAY

9:00 AM — 10:30 AM

Fill in these boxes and read what is printed below.

Full name of centre

Town

Forename(s)

Surname

Number of seat

Date of birth

Day Month Year

Scottish candidate number

Total marks — 20

Write your answer clearly, in **Spanish**, in the space provided in this booklet.

You may use a Spanish dictionary.

Additional space for answers is provided at the end of this booklet.

Use **blue** or **black** ink.

There is a separate question and answer booklet for Reading. You must complete your answers for Reading in the question and answer booklet for Reading.

Before leaving the examination room you must give both booklets to the Invigilator; if you do not, you may lose all the marks for this paper.

MARKS | DO NOT WRITE IN THIS MARGIN

Total marks — 20

You are preparing an application for the job advertised below and write an e-mail in **Spanish** to the company.

Buscamos recepcionista

Se necesita recepcionista para trabajar los fines de semana en un hotel en Madrid.

Preferiblemente con conocimientos básicos de inglés. Hay posibilidad de alojamiento en el hotel.

Los interesados deben mandar un email al director del hotel: carmen.arroyolopez@hotelsol.es

---

To help you to write your e-mail, you have been given the following checklist.

You must include **all** of these points:

- Personal details (name, age, where you live)
- School/college/education experience until now
- Skills/interests you have which make you right for the job
- Related work experience
- Your plans for accommodation in Madrid
- Why you want to work in Madrid.

Use all of the above to help you write the e-mail in **Spanish**. The e-mail should be approximately 120 —150 words. You may use a Spanish dictionary.

MARKS

DO NOT
WRITE IN
THIS
MARGIN

ANSWER SPACE

[Turn over

MARKS

DO NOT
WRITE IN
THIS
MARGIN

ANSWER SPACE (continued)

ANSWER SPACE (continued)

MARKS | DO NOT WRITE IN THIS MARGIN

ANSWER SPACE (continued)

[END OF QUESTION PAPER]

MARKS | DO NOT WRITE IN THIS MARGIN

ADDITIONAL SPACE FOR ANSWERS

ADDITIONAL SPACE FOR ANSWERS

N5

National
Qualifications
2014

Mark

X769/75/03

**Spanish
Listening**

FRIDAY, 30 MAY

10:50 AM — 11:15 AM (approx)

Fill in these boxes and read what is printed below.

Full name of centre

Town

Forename(s)

Surname

Number of seat

Date of birth

Day	Month	Year	Scottish candidate number
D D	M M	Y Y	

Total marks — 20

Attempt ALL questions

Write your answers clearly, in **English**, in the spaces provided in this booklet. Additional space for answers is provided at the end of this booklet. If you use this space you must clearly identify the question number you are attempting.

Use **blue** or **black** ink.

You will hear two items in Spanish. **Before you hear each item, you will have one minute to study the questions.** You will hear each item three times, with an interval of one minute between playings. You will then have time to answer the questions before hearing the next item.

You may take notes as you are listening to the Spanish, but only in this booklet.

You may NOT use a Spanish dictionary.

You are not allowed to leave the examination room until the end of the test.

Before leaving the examination room you must give this booklet to the Invigilator; if you do not, you may lose all the marks for this paper.

MARKS DO NOT WRITE IN THIS MARGIN

Total marks — 20

Attempt ALL questions

Item 1

Javier talks to us about whether or not he has a healthy lifestyle.

(a) What type of exercise does Javier do? State **two** things.   2

_____

_____

(b) Why does he avoid fast food? State any **one** thing.   1

_____

(c) Why does Javier's mum shop in the market? State any **one** thing.   1

_____

(d) Javier has one weakness, however. What is it? Complete the sentence.

Javier's problem is that he loves _____ .   1

(e) Why was Javier overweight when he was younger? State any **two** things.   2

_____

_____

(f) How would you describe Javier's attitude towards his health? Tick (✓) the correct statement.   1

He does lots to look after his health.	
He doesn't do much to look after his health.	
He doesn't care about his health.	

MARKS | DO NOT WRITE IN THIS MARGIN

Item 2

Sara talks to Javier about her lifestyle.

(a) What does Sara do to stay in shape? State any **one** thing.   1

_____

(b) What does she use her computer for? State any **two** things.   2

_____

_____

(c) What comment does Javier make about Sara's use of the computer?   1

_____

(d) (i) Sara talks about her parents' opinion of social networks. Complete the sentence.

Sara's parents think that social networks can be dangerous because

_____ .   1

(ii) In what way does Sara avoid problems with social networks?

_____   1

(e) Why does she send a lot of texts? State any **one** thing.   1

_____

(f) What else does she do on her phone apart from texting? State any **two** things.   2

_____

_____

[Turn over

MARKS | DO NOT WRITE IN THIS MARGIN

2. (continued)

    (g) Where does Sara go when she goes out? State **three** places.

        3

_____

_____

_____

[END OF QUESTION PAPER]

MARKS | DO NOT WRITE IN THIS MARGIN

ADDITIONAL SPACE FOR ANSWERS

MARKS DO NOT WRITE IN THIS MARGIN

ADDITIONAL SPACE FOR ANSWERS

National Qualifications 2014

X769/75/13

Spanish
Listening Transcript

FRIDAY, 30 MAY

10:50 AM — 11:15 AM (approx)

This paper must not be seen by any candidate.

The material overleaf is provided for use in an emergency only (eg the recording or equipment proving faulty) or where permission has been given in advance by SQA for the material to be read to candidates with additional support needs. The material must be read exactly as printed.

Instructions to reader(s):

For each item, read the English once, then read the Spanish three times, with an interval of 1 minute between the three readings. On completion of the third reading, pause for the length of time indicated in brackets after the item, to allow the candidates to write their answers.

Where special arrangements have been agreed in advance to allow the reading of the material, those sections marked **(f)** should be read by a female speaker and those marked **(m)** by a male; those sections marked **(t)** should be read by the teacher.

(t) Item Number One

Javier talks to us about whether or not he has a healthy lifestyle.

You now have one minute to study the questions.

(m) Primero, trato de llevar una vida sana. En general hago mucho ejercicio porque soy miembro de un equipo de baloncesto y también voy al gimnasio al menos una vez a la semana. Pienso que mi dieta es más o menos sana porque normalmente evito la comida rápida porque contiene mucha grasa y demasiada sal. Sé que tengo suerte porque todos los días, mi madre me prepara una cena equilibrada. Mi madre siempre hace la compra en el mercado para asegurarse que las verduras sean frescas y de buena calidad. Sin embargo, el problema es que me encantan las bebidas gaseosas – para mí son un verdadero placer pero sé que contienen demasiado azúcar. Hoy en día, me mantengo en forma, pero, cuando era niño, pesaba muchos más kilos. Me gustaba mucho la comida basura que ya no como nunca. Además, mis abuelos me daban pasteles cuando iba a visitarles a su casa. También, los fines de semana, mis amigos y yo solíamos comprar muchos caramelos con nuestro dinero.

(2 minutes)

(t) Item Number Two

Sara talks to Javier about her lifestyle.

You now have one minute to study the questions.

(m) Hola Sara, ¿qué haces para mantenerte en forma?

(f) ¡Hombre! No hago mucho para cuidarme la línea. A veces voy al polideportivo pero la verdad es que prefiero hacer otras cosas.

(m) ¡Ah vale! Entonces, ¿cómo prefieres pasar tus ratos libres?

(f) Uso mucho el ordenador en mi tiempo libre. Cuando vuelvo del instituto, me encanta conectarme para descargar las últimas canciones, chatear con amigos que no veo a menudo y a veces lo uso para buscar información para los deberes. Ya ves que lo encuentro útil.

(m) Claro que sí, pero me parece que pasas mucho tiempo usando el ordenador, ¿qué opinan tus padres?

(f) Mis padres se preocupan y dicen que las redes sociales pueden ser peligrosas porque mucha gente puede ver tu perfil. No estoy de acuerdo.

(m) Entonces, ¿qué piensas de eso?

(f) En mi opinión no hay ningún problema porque siempre mantengo mi perfil privado.

(m) ¡Buena idea! ¿Podrías vivir sin tu móvil?

(f) Pues no, porque lo necesito para mandar mensajes a mis amigos porque viven bastante lejos y no puedo salir mucho con ellos.

(m) Es una lástima. ¿Es un móvil inteligente?

(f) Sí, tengo un móvil nuevo y lo uso muchísimo. Aparte de mandar mensajes, leo páginas web sobre las personas famosas, y claro, muy a menudo, veo programas de televisión y, para organizarme, uso el calendario.

(m) Ah, yo también. Y cuando sales de casa, ¿adónde prefieres ir?

(f) Pues, siempre tengo que pasear el perro a lo largo de la playa todas las tardes, después del colegio. Los fines de semana, lo que más me gusta hacer es ir al centro comercial para ver lo que hay de nuevo en las tiendas. Cuando salgo con mis amigos, normalmente si hace buen tiempo tomamos unas copas en la plaza mayor.

(m) Pues nada, hasta la próxima.

(f) Vale, adiós.

(2 minutes)

(t) End of test.

Now look over your answers.

[END OF TRANSCRIPT]

[BLANK PAGE]

DO NOT WRITE ON THIS PAGE

NATIONAL 5

2015

Mark

N5

National
Qualifications
2015

X769/75/01

Spanish
Reading

FRIDAY, 29 MAY

9:00 AM – 10:30 AM

Fill in these boxes and read what is printed below.

Full name of centre

Town

Forename(s)

Surname

Number of seat

Date of birth

Day	Month	Year		Scottish candidate number

Total marks — 30

Attempt ALL questions.

Write your answers clearly, in **English**, in the spaces provided in this booklet.

You may use a Spanish dictionary.

Additional space for answers is provided at the end of this booklet. If you use this space you must clearly identify the question number you are attempting.

Use **blue** or **black** ink.

There is a separate question and answer booklet for Writing. You must complete your answer for Writing in the question and answer booklet for Writing.

Before leaving the examination room you must give both booklets to the Invigilator; if you do not, you may lose all the marks for this paper.

MARKS | DO NOT WRITE IN THIS MARGIN

Total marks — 30

Attempt ALL questions

Text 1

You read an article about young people and part-time jobs.

TRABAJAR Y ESTUDIAR CON 16 AÑOS

Como joven es probable que tengas algún tiempo libre y el deseo de ganar dinero. Además de ofrecerte una fuente de ingresos para tus gastos personales, el primer empleo te permitirá independizarte, y ver cómo funciona el mundo de los negocios.

Un poco de dinero extra siempre viene bien para salir de juerga con los amigos y para ahorrar para el carné de conducir. Sin embargo, compaginar estudios y trabajo es un desafío para muchos que no tienen tiempo de terminar todos los deberes del instituto. Los trabajos típicos incluyen rellenar estantes en el supermercado, repartir periódicos en el barrio o cuidar niños de los parientes.

Natalia Méndez Goya, de dieciséis años, dice: «*Pues yo gano dinero extra enseñando a mi abuelo de setenta y tres años a utilizar internet y antes de ir al colegio paseo los dos perros de mi vecino.*»

Se recomienda que los jóvenes no trabajen de noche durante la semana porque les resultará muy difícil levantarse temprano por la mañana para llegar al instituto a tiempo. Entre los jóvenes que trabajan por la noche, muchos van a clase dormidos o sin haber tenido tiempo de desayunar y por lo tanto no aprenden prácticamente nada.

Questions

(a) Complete the following sentence.

As a young person you will probably have some free time and _____

_____ .

1

(b) What will your first job allow you to do? State any **one** thing.

1

_____

MARKS | DO NOT WRITE IN THIS MARGIN

Text 1 Questions (continued)

(c) How can you spend extra money? State **two** things.   2

_____

_____

(d) What jobs do young people typically do? Give details of any **two**.   2

_____

_____

(e) Natalia Méndez Goya talks about her part-time jobs. What does she do
to earn extra money? State any **one** thing.   1

_____

_____

(f)   (i) Why should young people not work at night?   1

_____

(ii) What can happen to many young people who do work at night?
State any **one** thing.   1

_____

(g) What does the article say about part-time jobs? Tick (✓) the correct
box.   1

Having a part-time job while studying is something all young people should do.	
Having a part-time job while studying is difficult for many young people.	
Having a part-time job and studying is very popular in Spain.	

[Turn over

Text 2

You read an article about a museum in Madrid.

El Museo de Arte Moderno

El Museo de Arte Moderno en Madrid va a celebrar su quinto aniversario con unas jornadas de puertas abiertas. Se podrán visitar, con acceso gratuito, las nuevas esculturas norteamericanas. Además, se ha creado una exposición de arte moderno europeo.

Dolores Rodríguez, directora del museo, informa: "estamos seguros de que ofrecemos una gran selección de arte que a todos los visitantes les va a apasionar. Al visitar el museo, la gente puede descubrir a artistas menos conocidos además de mirar pinturas de los últimos cincuenta años."

El público también tendrá la oportunidad de participar en la celebración votando por su obra de arte favorita. Pueden dar su opinión a través de las pantallas táctiles en las salas del museo o rellenando una encuesta en la página web.

El horario será el habitual de lunes a sábado, de diez a siete horas de la tarde. Si las jornadas tienen mucho éxito, Dolores tiene planes de organizar más días de acceso gratuito para los jubilados.

Questions

(a) Which anniversary is the museum celebrating?

1

_____

(b) The museum is having a series of open days. What will people be able to visit? State **two** things.

2

_____

_____

MARKS | DO NOT WRITE IN THIS MARGIN

Text 2 Questions (continued)

(c) Dolores Rodríguez says the museum offers a large selection of art. According to Dolores, what will visitors think of it?

   1

_____

(d) What can people do during their visit? Complete the sentence.

   2

People can discover _____ and

they can look at paintings _____ .

(e) The public is encouraged to participate in the museum's anniversary.

    (i) How can they take part in the celebration?

   1

_____

_____

    (ii) How will they be able to give their opinion? State **two** things.

   2

_____

_____

(f) What plans does Dolores have for the museum?

   1

_____

_____

[Turn over

MARKS | DO NOT WRITE IN THIS MARGIN

Text 3

You read an article about facial recognition software which is being developed for use in cars.

El reconocimiento facial dentro del coche

La mayor parte de los accidentes de tráfico son debidos al conductor, por ejemplo si el conductor conduce con un exceso de velocidad o sin prudencia. Así que no es de extrañar que cada vez más fabricantes de automóviles trabajen en el desarrollo de una tecnología que emplea una cámara de vídeo y un *software* de reconocimiento facial para intentar mejorar la seguridad durante la conducción.

La cámara grabará los cambios de las expresiones faciales, movimientos musculares, y emociones del rostro del conductor. Además, el sistema tendrá que estar permanentemente vigilante para poder reconocer si el conductor está distraído, si está sufriendo somnolencia o si no está en condiciones de seguir conduciendo.

Hay alguna dificultad. Hay que buscar la mejor posición para la cámara para que tenga una buena visión del rostro del conductor.

Este sistema puede advertir al conductor de que no está en condiciones para conducir por hacer sonar una alarma cinco veces si está durmiendo.

No cabe duda alguna de que reducir los riesgos al factor humano de una manera tecnológica es positivo. Por ejemplo, puede ayudar al conductor a actuar para evitar un accidente.

Questions

(a) Complete the following sentence. 2

Most traffic accidents are the fault of the driver. For example if the driver

is driving _____ or _____ .

MARKS | DO NOT WRITE IN THIS MARGIN

Text 3 Questions (continued)

(b) What is the purpose of facial recognition software in cars?

_____

_____

1

(c) What will the camera record? State any **two** things.

_____

_____

2

(d) Why will the system have to be permanently switched on? State any **two** things.

_____

_____

2

(e) How can the system warn drivers? Give **two** details.

_____

_____

2

(f) According to the final paragraph, why is this type of technology positive?

_____

_____

1

[END OF QUESTION PAPER]

ADDITIONAL SPACE FOR ANSWERS

MARKS | DO NOT WRITE IN THIS MARGIN

ADDITIONAL SPACE FOR ANSWERS

[BLANK PAGE]

DO NOT WRITE ON THIS PAGE

N5

National
Qualifications
2015

Mark

X769/75/02

**Spanish
Writing**

FRIDAY, 29 MAY

9:00 AM – 10:30 AM

Fill in these boxes and read what is printed below.

Full name of centre

Town

Forename(s)

Surname

Number of seat

Date of birth

Day	Month	Year

Scottish candidate number

Total marks — 20

Write your answer clearly, in **Spanish**, in the space provided in this booklet.

You may use a Spanish dictionary.

Additional space for answers is provided at the end of this booklet.

Use **blue** or **black** ink.

There is a separate question and answer booklet for Reading. You must complete your answers for Reading in the question and answer booklet for Reading.

Before leaving the examination room you must give both booklets to the Invigilator; if you do not, you may lose all the marks for this paper.

MARKS | DO NOT WRITE IN THIS MARGIN

Total marks — 20

You are preparing an application for the job advertised below and you write an e-mail in **Spanish** to the company.

Se necesita dependiente/dependienta

Se requiere una persona seria, dinámica y responsable para trabajar en una tienda de ropa en Sevilla.

Imprescindible hablar inglés y preferiblemente otro idioma. Buena presencia esencial.

Se ruega escribir al director de la tienda:
manuel.garciaramirez@tiendaroja.es

To help you to write your e-mail, you have been given the following checklist.

You must include **all** of these points:

- Personal details (name, age, where you live)
- School/college/education experience until now
- Skills/interests you have which make you right for the job
- Related work experience
- Languages spoken
- Reasons for application

Use all of the above to help you write the e-mail in **Spanish**. The e-mail should be approximately 120—150 words. You may use a Spanish dictionary.

ANSWER SPACE

_____

_____

_____

_____

_____

_____

_____

_____

_____

_____

_____

_____

_____

_____

_____

_____

_____

_____

_____

_____

_____

_____

_____

_____

_____

_____

_____

[Turn over

ANSWER SPACE (continued)

MARKS

ANSWER SPACE (continued)

[Turn over

MARKS DO NOT WRITE IN THIS MARGIN

ANSWER SPACE (continued)

[END OF QUESTION PAPER]

MARKS | DO NOT WRITE IN THIS MARGIN

ADDITIONAL SPACE FOR ANSWERS

ADDITIONAL SPACE FOR ANSWERS

N5

National Qualifications 2015

Mark

X769/75/03

Spanish Listening

FRIDAY, 29 MAY

10:50 AM – 11:15 AM (approx)

Fill in these boxes and read what is printed below.

Full name of centre

Town

Forename(s)

Surname

Number of seat

Date of birth

Day   Month   Year

Scottish candidate number

Total marks — 20

Attempt ALL questions.

You will hear two items in Spanish. **Before you hear each item, you will have one minute to study the questions.** You will hear each item three times, with an interval of one minute between playings. You will then have time to answer the questions before hearing the next item.

You may NOT use a Spanish dictionary.

Write your answers clearly, in **English**, in the spaces provided in this booklet. Additional space for answers is provided at the end of this booklet. If you use this space you must clearly identify the question number you are attempting.

Use **blue** or **black** ink.

You are not allowed to leave the examination room until the end of the test.

Before leaving the examination room you must give this booklet to the Invigilator; if you do not, you may lose all the marks for this paper.

MARKS

DO NOT WRITE IN THIS MARGIN

Total marks — 20

Attempt ALL questions

Item 1

Luisa talks about languages.

(a) What does Luisa say about her mum? State any **one** thing.

1

_____

(b) What makes Luisa's English classes fun? State any **one** thing.

1

_____

(c) Apart from computers, what other kind of technology does she use in her English class?

1

_____

(d) Luisa talks about the advantage of speaking different languages. What does she say?

1

_____

(e) Luisa went to a summer camp last year. Where did she go?

1

_____

(f) What does she want to do when she finishes her studies? State **two** things.

2

_____

_____

(g) Which statement best matches Luisa's attitude to languages? Tick (✓) the correct statement.

1

She really likes them but they are just another school subject.	
She thinks they are good for holidays.	
They play an important part in many areas of her life.	

Item 2

Francisco talks to Luisa about his exams.

MARKS

(a) How much time does Francisco spend revising?

1

_____

(b) He gives details of the exam timetable. Tick (✓) the **two** correct statements.

2

The exams start the next day.	
The first exam is Biology.	
The exams finish on the 12th of June.	
They last for 17 days in total.	

(c) Why does he prefer studying with a friend? State any **two** things.

2

_____

_____

(d) How does he relax when he has a break? State any **two** things.

2

_____

_____

(e) What does he find difficult about History?

1

_____

(f) Francisco says the weather is nice. What would he rather be doing? State any **two** things.

2

_____

_____

(g) Francisco is anxious about his Maths exam. Why? State any **two** things.

2

_____

_____

[END OF QUESTION PAPER]

MARKS DO NOT WRITE IN THIS MARGIN

ADDITIONAL SPACE FOR ANSWERS

ADDITIONAL SPACE FOR ANSWERS

Page five

[BLANK PAGE]

DO NOT WRITE ON THIS PAGE

National Qualifications 2015

X769/75/13

Spanish Listening Transcript

FRIDAY, 29 MAY

10:50 AM — 11:15 AM (approx)

This paper must not be seen by any candidate.

The material overleaf is provided for use in an emergency only (eg the recording or equipment proving faulty) or where permission has been given in advance by SQA for the material to be read to candidates with additional support needs. The material must be read exactly as printed.

Instructions to reader(s)

For each item, read the English **once**, then read the Spanish **three times**, with an interval of 1 minute between the three readings. On completion of the third reading, pause for the length of time indicated in brackets after the item, to allow the candidates to write their answers.

Where special arrangements have been agreed in advance to allow the reading of the material, those sections marked **(f)** should be read by a female speaker and those marked **(m)** by a male; those sections marked **(t)** should be read by the teacher.

(t)   **Item Number One**

Luisa talks about languages.

You now have one minute to study the questions for Item Number One.

(f)   Siempre me han interesado los idiomas. Creo que es porque mi madre es suiza y habla muchas lenguas . . . francés, italiano y alemán.

Además, este año tengo suerte porque en el colegio tenemos una profesora de inglés que es muy entusiasta. Sus clases son muy divertidas – aprendemos canciones y ella tiene muy buen sentido del humor. También, utilizo la tecnología a menudo, es decir los ordenadores y la pizarra interactiva así que las clases son muy interesantes. Una ventaja de aprender lenguas es que puedo ayudar a muchos de los turistas extranjeros que visitan mi ciudad cada año.

El año pasado pasé un mes en un campamento de verano en la costa este de Irlanda – me lo pasé de maravilla y mi inglés ha mejorado mucho.

He decidido que cuando termine mis estudios quisiera encontrar trabajo en una empresa internacional y viajar por todo el mundo.

Lo tengo muy claro, todos los jóvenes deberían hablar una lengua además de la materna.

(2 minutes)

(t)   **Item Number Two**

     Francisco talks to Luisa about his exams.

     You now have one minute to study the questions for Item Number Two.

(f)   Hace mucho que no te veo, Francisco . . . ¿qué tal?

(m)   En este momento estoy preparando mis exámenes de fin de curso. Cada tarde paso tres horas repasando mis asignaturas.

(f)   Y ¿cuándo son estos exámenes?

(m)   Empiezan el martes por la mañana . . . el primero es biología. Terminan el 11 de junio con informática. Así que en total duran 17 días. ¡Qué tostón!

(f)   No es fácil trabajar solo ¿verdad?

(m)   Tienes razón, pero a veces mi amigo Vicente viene a mi casa y trabajamos juntos, creo que aprendo mejor, el tiempo pasa más rápido y no me aburro tanto.

(f)   Pero es importante también tomarse un descanso de vez en cuando ¿no?

(m)   Sí, sí . . . me tomo un descanso cada hora para comer unas galletas, llamar a mis amigos o mirar una telenovela durante diez minutos . . . depende.

(f)   Y estudiar ¿te parece fácil?

(m)   Para mí lo más difícil es la historia, me cuesta mucho memorizar las fechas importantes.

(f)   Sí . . . pero creo que es igual para todo el mundo.

(m)   Lo peor es que en este momento hace buen tiempo y me gustaría estar al aire libre para dar una vuelta en bici o entrenarme con mi club de natación. Pero no hay más remedio.

(f)   Bueno, por lo menos pareces muy relajado.

(m)   ¡No! El miércoles tengo exámen de matemáticas. Estoy un poco preocupado porque creo que no he trabajado bastante en clase. Además, no me siento muy bien y me duele un poco la garganta. ¡Ojalá que todo salga bien!

(2 minutes)

(t)   **End of test.**

     Now look over your answers.

[END OF TRANSCRIPT]

[BLANK PAGE]

DO NOT WRITE ON THIS PAGE

NATIONAL 5

2016

N5

National
Qualifications
2016

Mark

X769/75/01

**Spanish
Reading**

THURSDAY, 26 MAY

1:00 PM – 2:30 PM

Fill in these boxes and read what is printed below.

Full name of centre

Town

Forename(s)

Surname

Number of seat

Date of birth

Day   Month   Year   Scottish candidate number

Total marks — 30

Attempt ALL questions.

Write your answers clearly, in **English**, in the spaces provided in this booklet.

You may use a Spanish dictionary.

Additional space for answers is provided at the end of this booklet. If you use this space you must clearly identify the question number you are attempting.

Use **blue** or **black** ink.

There is a separate question and answer booklet for Writing. You must complete your answer for Writing in the question and answer booklet for Writing.

Before leaving the examination room you must give both booklets to the Invigilator; if you do not, you may lose all the marks for this paper.

MARKS | DO NOT WRITE IN THIS MARGIN

Total marks — 30

Attempt ALL questions

Text 1

You read an article about a beach clean-up.

> ## Cuarenta voluntarios para limpiar la playa
>
>
>
> Unos cuarenta voluntarios trabajaron ayer para limpiar la playa de Sant Antoni en Ibiza. Los voluntarios al final de la jornada llenaron más de cincuenta bolsas con basura. El grupo, formado tanto por personas jóvenes como por familias, se reunió sobre las diez de la mañana en la playa.
>
> Para algunos, como Carlos Aguado, era la primera vez que participaban. Carlos decidió participar en el voluntariado al ver el daño que ha sufrido la costa estos últimos años. Después de la limpieza, Carlos comentaba que "Lo que más he encontrado son colillas, vidrio roto y bolsas de supermercado".
>
> La jornada de limpieza también contó con el apoyo de los turistas. Una pareja británica, tras enterarse de esta campaña, decidió ayudar: "Queremos proteger la belleza de la playa."
>
> El objetivo de esta limpieza es concienciar a la gente sobre la importancia de no tirar los residuos al mar. "No esperábamos a tanta gente", explicó Eva Marqués, organizadora. "En mi opinión, creo que el medio ambiente interesa a mucha gente", añadió. Después de este éxito, es seguro que en el futuro Eva organizará jornadas de limpieza en los parques y visitas escolares para informar a los alumnos.

Questions

(a) (i) How much rubbish did the volunteers collect from the beach? 1

_____

_____

MARKS | DO NOT WRITE IN THIS MARGIN

Text 1 Questions (continued)

    (ii) At what time did the group meet?   1

_____

_____

(b) For Carlos Aguado, it was his first time cleaning up the beach.

    (i) What did Carlos see that made him decide to participate?   1

_____

_____

    (ii) What sort of rubbish does he say he found? Give details of any **two** things.   2

_____

_____

(c) Some tourists also took part in the clean-up. Why did a British couple decide to help? Give details.   1

_____

_____

(d) Complete the sentence.   1

The purpose of this beach clean-up is to make people aware of the

importance of not _____

_____ .

(e) Eva Marqués organised the clean-up.

    (i) Why does Eva think that so many people turned up?   1

_____

_____

    (ii) What will she organise in the future? State **two** things.   2

_____

_____

MARKS | DO NOT WRITE IN THIS MARGIN

Text 2

You read an article about International Girls' Day.

El Día Internacional de la Niña

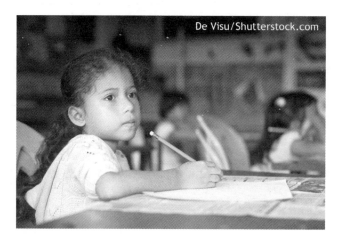

De Visu/Shutterstock.com

Según una organización internacional, muchas niñas en varios paises del mundo hacen frente al problema de la falta de educación. Las Naciones Unidas han declarado el 11 de octubre como Día Internacional de la Niña.

El objetivo del Día Internacional de la Niña es de reconocer los derechos de las niñas, de intentar solucionar los problemas excepcionales que enfrentan las niñas, y de aumentar la proporción de niñas que completan la educación básica.

75 millones de niñas no van al colegio

Un estudio reciente demuestra que un tercio de niñas en el mundo no completa la educación secundaria y el 24 por ciento de las mujeres son analfabetas.

Muchas niñas se incorporan a la fuerza laboral a una edad temprana y suelen hacer los trabajos peor remunerados y menos valorados, por ejemplo en el servicio doméstico.

Un futuro optimista en El Salvador

Con el apoyo internacional, la vida de más de 5000 niñas de El Salvador ha mejorado muchísimo porque han podido estudiar un año más. Como resultado tienen la posibilidad de acceder a mejores empleos y de generar más ingresos para sus familias.

MARKS | DO NOT WRITE IN THIS MARGIN

Questions

(a) According to an international organisation, what problem do many girls face?

1

_____

_____

(b) What is the aim of International Girls' Day? State any **two** things.

2

_____

_____

(c) Complete the sentence.

2

According to a recent study, a third of girls in the world _____

_____

and 24% of women are _____ .

(d) Many girls join the work force at an early age. What types of jobs do girls often do? State any **two**.

2

_____

_____

(e) In what **three** ways have the lives of more than 5000 girls in El Salvador improved?

3

_____

_____

_____

[Turn over

MARKS | DO NOT WRITE IN THIS MARGIN

Text 3

You read an article about the increase in people working from home.

Trabajar desde casa

Cada vez son más los empleados que "teletrabajan", o sea, que trabajan en casa. Este método de trabajar desde fuera de la oficina es aún más popular en España impulsado por mejor acceso a Internet y las tecnologías de la comunicación.

Además de reportar beneficios económicos, puede aumentar la productividad para las empresas. Y, para los trabajadores, trabajar a distancia permite que se pueda equilibrar la vida laboral con la vida familiar.

Elena Torres es técnico de recursos humanos. Lleva más de tres años teletrabajando para su compañía y está satisfecha con el sistema de teletrabajo. Dice: "Me conecto a Internet para estar comunicada constantemente con mis compañeros. Y puedo hacerlo desde casa o, entre cita y cita, desde un café o un parque."

De lunes a viernes, Elena sigue exactamente la misma rutina diaria: se levanta bastante temprano, toma su desayuno mientras lee su correo electrónico, se viste con ropa cómoda y anda un par de pasos hasta el salón de su casa.

"Gracias al teletrabajo, mi vida ha mejorado mucho. Me organizo el tiempo a mi manera", resume.

Questions

(a) Working at home is becoming more popular in Spain. What **two** reasons does the article give for this?

2

_____

_____

MARKS | DO NOT WRITE IN THIS MARGIN

Text 3 Questions (continued)

(b) The article describes the benefits of working from home.

    (i) As well as economic benefits, what is the other advantage for companies?

      1

_____

_____

    (ii) What is the main benefit for workers?

      1

_____

_____

(c) Elena Torres explains why she is satisfied with this way of working. What does she say? State any **two** things.

    2

_____

_____

_____

(d) She describes her daily routine from Monday to Friday. What does she say? State any **three** things.

    3

_____

_____

_____

(e) What does Elena think about working from home? Tick (✓) the correct statement.

    1

	Tick (✓)
Working from home has made her life more comfortable.	
Working from home can be difficult.	
Working from home has many advantages.	

[END OF QUESTION PAPER]

ADDITIONAL SPACE FOR ANSWERS

MARKS | DO NOT WRITE IN THIS MARGIN

ADDITIONAL SPACE FOR ANSWERS

[BLANK PAGE]

DO NOT WRITE ON THIS PAGE

N5

National Qualifications 2016

Mark

X769/75/02

Spanish Writing

THURSDAY, 26 MAY
1:00 PM – 2:30 PM

Fill in these boxes and read what is printed below.

Full name of centre

Town

Forename(s)

Surname

Number of seat

Date of birth

Day	Month	Year		Scottish candidate number

Total marks — 20

Write your answer clearly, in **Spanish**, in the space provided in this booklet.

You may use a Spanish dictionary.

Additional space for answers is provided at the end of this booklet.

Use **blue** or **black** ink.

There is a separate question and answer booklet for Reading. You must complete your answers for Reading in the question and answer booklet for Reading.

Before leaving the examination room you must give both booklets to the Invigilator; if you do not, you may lose all the marks for this paper.

Total marks — 20

You are preparing an application for the job advertised below and you write an e-mail in **Spanish** to the company.

Buscamos camarero/a

La heladería 'El Cucurucho', necesita **camarero/a** con conocimiento perfecto del inglés para este verano.

Las responsabilidades principales serán: preparar y servir los helados caseros en nuestro renombrado salón.

Se requiere una persona trabajadora con excelentes habilidades para la comunicación.

Envía tu currículum a *elcucurucho@heladerÍa.es*

To help you to write your e-mail, you have been given the following checklist.

You must include **all** of these points:

- Personal details (name, age, where you live)
- School/college/education experience until now
- Skills/interests you have which make you right for the job
- Related work experience
- When you are available to work in the summer
- Your future career plans

Use all of the above to help you write the e-mail in **Spanish**. The e-mail should be approximately 120–150 words. You may use a Spanish dictionary.

MARKS | DO NOT WRITE IN THIS MARGIN

ANSWER SPACE

ANSWER SPACE (continued)

MARKS | DO NOT WRITE IN THIS MARGIN

ANSWER SPACE (continued)

MARKS | DO NOT WRITE IN THIS MARGIN

ANSWER SPACE (continued)

[END OF QUESTION PAPER]

MARKS | DO NOT WRITE IN THIS MARGIN

ADDITIONAL SPACE FOR ANSWERS

MARKS DO NOT WRITE IN THIS MARGIN

ADDITIONAL SPACE FOR ANSWERS

N5

National
Qualifications
2016

Mark

X769/75/03

**Spanish
Listening**

THURSDAY, 26 MAY

2:50 PM – 3:20 PM (approx)

Fill in these boxes and read what is printed below.

Full name of centre

Town

Forename(s)

Surname

Number of seat

Date of birth

| Day | Month | Year | Scottish candidate number |

Total marks — 20

Attempt ALL questions.

You will hear two items in Spanish. **Before you hear each item, you will have one minute to study the questions.** You will hear each item three times, with an interval of one minute between playings. You will then have time to answer the questions before hearing the next item.

You may NOT use a Spanish dictionary.

Write your answers clearly, in **English**, in the spaces provided in this booklet. Additional space for answers is provided at the end of this booklet. If you use this space you must clearly identify the question number you are attempting.

Use **blue** or **black** ink.

You are not allowed to leave the examination room until the end of the test.

Before leaving the examination room you must give this booklet to the Invigilator; if you do not, you may lose all the marks for this paper.

MARKS | DO NOT WRITE IN THIS MARGIN

Total marks — 20

Attempt ALL questions

Item 1

Gabriela talks about reading.

(a) Complete the table.   2

When does she read?	For how long?
	Half an hour
Every evening	

(b) When she was a child, who read poems and stories to her?   1

_____

(c) What does she now prefer to read?   1

_____

(d) Why does she not like science fiction novels? State any **one** thing.   1

_____

(e) Gabriela uses her tablet for reading. What else does she use it for? State **two** things.   2

_____

_____

(f) Which statement best describes Gabriela's reason for reading? Tick (✓) the correct statement.   1

	Tick (✓)
She reads to help her with her school work.	
She reads for enjoyment.	
She reads when she is bored.	

[Turn over for next question

DO NOT WRITE ON THIS PAGE

MARKS | DO NOT WRITE IN THIS MARGIN

Item 2

Ana tells Javi about the International Music Festival of Benicàssim.

(a) When did Ana first go to the Benicàssim Festival?   1

_____

(b) How long does the festival last?   1

_____

(c) What does Ana like most about the festival?   1

_____

_____

(d) Apart from the concerts, what else does the festival have to offer? State any **two** things.   2

_____

_____

(e) There is also a free camping zone at the festival. What can you do there? State **two** things.   2

_____

_____

(f) Ana talks about where she stayed the last time she went to the festival.

   (i) Why did she not go camping?   1

   _____

   _____

   (ii) Where did she stay? Give any **one** detail.   1

   _____

   _____

MARKS | DO NOT WRITE IN THIS MARGIN

Item 2 (continued)

(g) Why are her parents allowing her to go with her friends this year? Give any **two** reasons.

2

_____

_____

(h) What is Ana most looking forward to about the festival? Tick (✓) the correct statement.

1

	Tick (✓)
Staying in the campsite.	
Enjoying the atmosphere.	
Being away without her parents.	
Seeing her favourite band.	

[END OF QUESTION PAPER]

ADDITIONAL SPACE FOR ANSWERS

Page six

MARKS | DO NOT WRITE IN THIS MARGIN

ADDITIONAL SPACE FOR ANSWERS

[BLANK PAGE]

DO NOT WRITE ON THIS PAGE

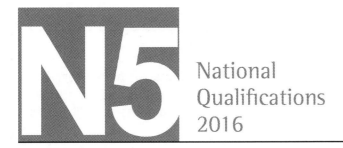

National Qualifications 2016

X769/75/13

Spanish
Listening Transcript

THURSDAY, 26 MAY
2:50 PM – 3:20 PM (approx)

This paper must not be seen by any candidate.

The material overleaf is provided for use in an emergency only (eg the recording or equipment proving faulty) or where permission has been given in advance by SQA for the material to be read to candidates with additional support needs. The material must be read exactly as printed.

Instructions to reader(s)

For each item, read the English **once**, then read the Spanish **three times**, with an interval of 1 minute between the three readings. On completion of the third reading, pause for the length of time indicated in brackets after the item, to allow the candidates to write their answers.

Where special arrangements have been agreed in advance to allow the reading of the material, those sections marked **(f)** should be read by a female speaker and those marked **(m)** by a male; those sections marked **(t)** should be read by the teacher.

(t) Item Number One

Gabriela talks about reading.

You now have one minute to study the questions for Item Number One.

(f) Suelo pasar mucho tiempo leyendo, tanto libro en papel como digital. Leo media hora por la mañana cuando me levanto y una hora y media cada tarde. Claro, los fines de semana puedo pasar todo el día leyendo, tumbada en el sofá con mi tablet. Cuando era niña, pasaba mucho tiempo con mi abuelo y él me leía poemas y cuentos infantiles. Ahora, leo de todo pero diría que mi tipo de novela preferida es la novela romántica. Sin embargo, a mí las novelas de ciencia-ficción no me gustan nada — las encuentro un poco aburridas y no son realistas. No entiendo a la gente que no lee nunca. Además de leer en mi tablet, descargo aplicaciones y a veces, compro por Internet. ¡No puedo imaginar la vida sin mi tablet!

(2 minutes)

(t) Item Number Two

Ana tells Javi about the International Music Festival of Benicàssim.

You now have one minute to study the questions for Item Number Two.

(m) Oye Ana, ¿tienes planes para el verano?

(f) Bueno, hace dos años fui con mi familia por primera vez al Festival Internacional de Benicàssim y he decidido volver este año.

(m) ¡Qué interesante! ¿Qué tipo de festival es?

(f) Um bueno, es un festival de música que dura cuatro días y ofrece música en directo.

(m) Ah, y ¿qué tipos de música hay?

(f) Hay de todo. Todo tipo de música.

(m) Y ¿qué es lo que más te gusta?

(f) Bueno, lo que más me gusta es que puedo ver artistas y grupos diferentes en el mismo día. Es fenomenal.

(m) Oye pues me gustaría ir. Me parece que no me aburriría nada.

(f) Claro que no. El festival no se limita a ofrecer conciertos. Además, hay cine, teatro, concursos, baile y exposiciones.

(m) Es verdad que hay algo para todo el mundo.

(f) Sí. Incluso hay una zona de acampada gratuita donde se puede descansar y conocer gente de todo el mundo.

(m) Suena estupendo. ¿Tú acampaste?

(f) La última vez, no. Fui con mis padres y no les gusta acampar. Por eso, nos alojamos en la casa de mi tío. Tiene una casa en el centro de un pueblo cercano.

(m) Y este año, ¿vas a ir otra vez con la familia?

(f) Um no. Con la familia, no. Me voy con un grupo de amigos. Mis padres dicen que ahora soy mayor y confían en mí. También soy más independiente. Por eso mis padres me van a dejar ir con mis amigos. ¡Qué bien!

(m) Será fenomenal.

(f) Seguro que sí. Lo que más espero es disfrutar del ambiente. Porque han anunciado unos grupos de maravilla.

(2 minutes)

(t) End of test.

Now look over your answers.

[END OF TRANSCRIPT]

Page three

[BLANK PAGE]

DO NOT WRITE ON THIS PAGE

NATIONAL 5 SPANISH
2014

Reading

1. (a) • Travelling/(desire/wanting) to travel
     • Living in another European country/other parts of Europe/live in Europe

   (b) (i) A big change in her life/a big change in her lifestyle/it changed her life greatly

       (ii) • (Discovered) a new city
            • (Discovered) a different city (to hers)
            • She visited places (around Brussels)/she visited the surroundings
            • She experienced/soaked up/absorbed another culture
            • She had a great/good time/it was good
            Any two of the above

   (c) • (Went home) knowing/learnt/could speak/talk English
       • (Another) education system
       • Be in contact with/got to know/got connected to/have/make relationships with other people
       Any two of the above

   (d) (i) • No day was the same (as the last)/every day was different/no 2 days were the same
           • There was/he <u>always</u> had something to do/there was lots to do
       (ii) • Way of seeing/his view of/how he saw the world

2. (a) • Acted/performed/actor in the theatre
       • He starred/acted in his first soap opera/at 11 he starred in a soap opera

   (b) (i) (It had a lot of) international success/hit

       (ii) • Political
            • Funny
            • (Very) emotional/exciting/moving
       Any two of the above

   (c) • Promoting/helping Oxfam's campaigns/Promoting Oxfam/Campaigning/campaigns for Oxfam
       • The (most) vulnerable (population/people)

   (d) • How difficult life was for the farmers/difficulties of being a farmer/difficult (time) to be a farmer/life was difficult for farmers
       • Farmers complain about the unfair trade/commercial system
       Any one of the above

   (e) • Went to meetings
       • Discussed ideas
       • Presented case studies
       • Talked to the Media
       • Handed in/out/over delivered petitions
       Any two of the above

3. (a) • Advertising/publicity/commercials
       • Business/commerce/industry
       • Communication/to communicate
       Any two of the above

   (b) • A good/better reputation
       • Business/commercial contacts/links

   (c) • Use/go on databases
       • Find information on the Internet/Web

   (d) • Apps and programmes/used in applications and programmes

   (e) • Deal with/face up to problems
       • Start projects
       • Solving (unforeseen/unexpected) difficulties/Finding a solution to (unforeseen/unexpected) difficulties
       • Get on with colleagues/workmates/be a team player
       Any two of the above

   (f) • It gives you advice on what skills you need in a job
       Box 2

Writing

Candidates will write a piece of extended writing in the modern language by addressing six bullet points. These bullet points will follow on from a job-related scenario. The bullet points will cover the four contexts of society, learning, employability and culture to allow candidates to use and adapt learned material. The first four bullet points will be the same each year and the last two will change to suit the scenario. Candidates need to address these "unpredictable bullet points" in detail to access the full range of marks.

Category	Mark	Content	Accuracy	Language resource — variety, range, structures
Very good	20	The job advert has been addressed in a full and balanced way. The candidate uses detailed language. The candidate addresses the advert completely and competently, **including information in response to both unpredictable bullet points**. A range of verbs/ verb forms, tenses and constructions is used. Overall this comes over as a competent, well thought-out and serious application for the job.	The candidate handles all aspects of grammar and spelling accurately, although the language may contain one or two minor errors. Where the candidate attempts to use language more appropriate to Higher, a slightly higher number of inaccuracies need not detract from the overall very good impression.	The candidate is comfortable with the first person of the verb and generally uses a different verb in each sentence. Some modal verbs and infinitives may be used. There is good use of adjectives, adverbs and prepositional phrases and, where appropriate, word order. There may be a range of tenses. The candidate uses co-ordinating conjunctions and/or subordinate clauses where appropriate. The language of the e-mail flows well.
Good	16	The job advert has been addressed competently. There is less evidence of detailed language. The candidate uses a reasonable range of verbs/verb forms. Overall, the candidate has produced a genuine, reasonably accurate attempt at applying for the specific job, **even though he/she may not address one of the unpredictable bullet points**.	The candidate handles a range of verbs fairly accurately. There are some errors in spelling, adjective endings and, where relevant, case endings. Use of accents is less secure, where appropriate. Where the candidate is attempting to use more complex vocabulary and structures, these may be less successful, although basic structures are used accurately. There may be one or two examples of inaccurate dictionary use, especially in the unpredictable bullet points.	There may be repetition of verbs. There may be examples of listing, in particular when referring to school/ college experience, without further amplification. There may be one or two examples of a co-ordinating conjunction, but most sentences are simple sentences. The candidate keeps to more basic vocabulary, particularly in response to either or both unpredictable bullet points.

Category	Mark	Content	Accuracy	Language resource — variety, range, structures
Satisfactory	12	The job advert has been addressed fairly competently. The candidate makes limited use of detailed language. The language is fairly repetitive and uses a limited range of verbs and fixed phrases, eg I *like*, I *go*, I *play*. The candidate copes fairly well with areas of personal details, education, skills, interests and work experience but does not deal fully with the two unpredictable bullet points **and indeed may not address either or both of the unpredictable bullet points.** On balance however the candidate has produced a satisfactory job application in the specific language.	The verbs are generally correct, but may be repetitive. There are quite a few errors in other parts of speech — gender of nouns, cases, singular/plural confusion, for instance. Prepositions may be missing, eg I *go the town*. Overall, there is more correct than incorrect.	The candidate copes with the first and third person of a few verbs, where appropriate. A limited range of verbs is used. Sentences are basic and mainly brief. There is minimal use of adjectives, probably mainly after *is* eg *Chemistry is interesting*. The candidate has a weak knowledge of plurals. There may be several spelling errors, eg reversal of vowel combinations.
Unsatisfactory	8	The job advert has been addressed in an uneven manner and/or with insufficient use of detailed language. The language is repetitive, eg I *like*, I *go*, I *play* may feature several times. There may be little difference between Satisfactory and Unsatisfactory. **Either or both of the unpredictable bullet points may not have been addressed.** There may be one sentence which is not intelligible to a sympathetic native speaker.	Ability to form tenses is inconsistent. There are errors in many other parts of speech — gender of nouns, cases, singular/plural confusion, for instance. Several errors are serious, perhaps showing mother tongue interference. The detail in the unpredictable bullet points may be very weak. Overall, there is more incorrect than correct.	The candidate copes mainly only with the personal language required in bullet points 1 and 2. The verbs "is" and "study" may also be used correctly. Sentences are basic. An English word may appear in the writing. There may be an example of serious dictionary misuse.

Category	Mark	Content	Accuracy	Language resource — variety, range, structures
Poor	4	The candidate has had considerable difficulty in addressing the job advert. There is little evidence of the use of detailed language. Three or four sentences may not be understood by a sympathetic native speaker. **Either or both of the unpredictable bullet points may not have been addressed.**	Many of the verbs are incorrect. There are many errors in other parts of speech — personal pronouns, gender of nouns, cases, singular/plural confusion, prepositions, for instance. The language is probably inaccurate throughout the writing.	The candidate cannot cope with more than one or two basic verbs. The candidate displays almost no knowledge of the present tense of verbs. Verbs used more than once may be written differently on each occasion. Sentences are very short. The candidate has a very limited vocabulary. Several English words may appear in the writing. There are examples of serious dictionary misuse.
Very poor	0	The candidate is unable to address the job advert. **The two unpredictable bullet points may not have been addressed.** Very little is intelligible to a sympathetic native speaker.	Virtually nothing is correct.	The candidate may only cope with the verbs *to have* and *to be*. Very few words are written correctly in the modern language. English words are used. There may be several examples of mother tongue interference. There may be several examples of serious dictionary misuse.

Listening

Item 1

(a) • Basketball
• (He goes to the) gym.

(b) • (It contains) a lot of/too much grease/fat/it is very fatty/very greasy
• (It contains) too much/a lot of salt
Any one of the above

(c) • The vegetables are fresh
• The vegetables are good quality
Any one of the above

(d) fizzy drinks/fizzy juice

(e) • Liked/ate junk/fast food/rubbish
• His grandparents gave/made him cakes
• He (and his friends) bought sweets/caramels
Any two of the above

(f) He does lots to look after his health
(Box 1)

Item 2

(a) • Not much/not a lot
• (She goes to) the sports centre/leisure centre/sports hall
Any one of the above

(b) • Download songs
• Chat/talk to her friends
• Information for her homework/school work
Any two of the above

(c) She spends a lot of/too much time (using/on/the computer/online/on it)

(d) (i) (Many) people can see your profile

(ii) She keeps her profile/details/information private/to herself/hidden

(e) • Her friends live far away/doesn't live near her friends
• She can't/doesn't go out with/see/meet her friends much
Any one of the above

(f) • Reads about celebrities/searches famous people.
• Television/watches programmes
• Calendar
Any two of the above

(g) • Beach
• The shopping centre/mall/shops
• (Main/town/city) square

Reading

Text 1

(a) Want/wish/desire/need money
NB: Should have feeling of desire

(b) *Any one from:*
• Become/be independent
• Explore/see world of work/business
• Source of income

(c) • Go out to party/go out in the town/binge with friends
• Driving lessons/licence/test **or** to learn to drive

(d) *Any two from:*
• Stacking shelves in a supermarket
• Delivering papers/paper round
• Looking after/babysitting relatives' children

(e) *Any one from:*
• Teaches/helps her grandfather how to use the internet/go online
• Walks her neighbour's dogs

(f) (i) It's difficult to get up early/in the morning/for school

(ii) *Any one from:*
• Go to school/class tired/sleepy/fall asleep in class
• Don't have time for/skip breakfast
• Learn hardly anything/learn nothing

(g) **MIDDLE BOX** — Having a part-time job while studying is difficult for many young people
NB: If more than one box is ticked, 0 marks are awarded.

Text 2

(a) Fifth/5

(b) • American sculptures
• Modern European art (in any order)

(c) They are going to love it/go crazy about it/go wild for it/be passionate about it/it will excite them

(d) • Less well-known/less famous artists
• Of the last 50 years/50 years old/from 50 years ago

(e) (i) Voting for/choosing their favourite work of art/art/painting

(ii) • Touch/interactive/tactile screens
• Survey/questionnaire/evaluation online/on the webpage

(f) Free days/open days/free access for retired people/pensioners/retired citizens/senior citizens

Text 3

(a) • Fast/quickly/at excess speed
• Carelessly/without care/not sensibly/not wisely
NB: Accept responses in any order

(b) (To improve) safety

(c) *Any two from:*
• Facial expressions
• Muscle movements
• Emotions on the face

(d) *Any two from:*
- If the driver is distracted/absent minded/not concentrating
- If the driver is sleepy/drowsy/tired
- If the driver is not in a condition to drive
NB: The driver only needs to be mentioned once

(e) • Sound/set off an alarm 5 times
- If s/he is sleeping/asleep

(f) *Any one from:*
- Avoids/prevents an accident
- Reduces risks (of human error)

Writing

Please see the assessment criteria for Writing on pages 102–104.

Listening

Item 1

(a) *Any one from:*
- Swiss/from Switzerland
- Speaks/knows/understands many/lots of languages
- Speaks French, Italian and German **(any 2 languages)**

(b) *Any one from:*
- She has an enthusiastic teacher
- (Learns/sings) songs
- Teacher has good sense of humour
NB: Ignore gender

(c) Interactive board/Smart board/active board/ interactive screens/touch screens

(d) She helps/talks to/speaks to/communicates with tourists (visiting her town)

(e) Ireland
NB: Ignore wrong compass point

(f) • Work for an international company/business/firm/ office
- Travel/see/go around the world

(g) **BOTTOM BOX** — they play an important part in many areas of her life
NB: If more than one box is ticked, 0 marks are awarded.

Item 2

(a) Three hours
NB: Ignore additional information

(b) • **BOX 2** — the first exam is Biology
- **BOX 4** — they last for 17 days in total
NB: If three boxes ticked, maximum 1 mark; if four boxes ticked, 0 marks are awarded.

(c) *Any two from:*
- It's not easy working alone
- Learns better/more
- Time passes quicker/quickly/fast/faster
- Not so bored/not boring

(d) *Any two from:*
- Eats biscuits
- Calls/phones/talks/speaks to/chats with friends
- Watches a soap opera/TV series/TV drama

(e) (Remembering/memorising/learning) the dates

(f) *Any two from:*
- Be/go/relax outdoors/outside/in the open air/out in fresh air
- Going out on his bike/cycling
- Training with his swimming club/swimming

(g) *Any two from:*
- It's on Wednesday
- He hasn't worked (enough)/he hasn't done enough
- He is not feeling well/feels ill/feels sick
- He has a sore throat

NATIONAL 5 SPANISH 2016

Reading

Question			Expected Answer(s)	Max Mark
1.	(a)	(i)	<u>over/more than</u> 50 bags/bin bags	1
		(ii)	(around) 10am/10 in the morning	1
	(b)	(i)	damage (to the coast)	1
		(ii)	• cigarette butts/ends • broken/smashed/pieces of glass • supermarket bags **(Any 2 from 3)**	2
	(c)		protect/maintain the beauty of the beach(es)/keep the beach beautiful	1
	(d)		throwing/dropping waste/rubbish into the sea/ocean/water	1
	(e)	(i)	the environment interests them/they are interested in the environment	1
		(ii)	• park clean-ups/clear-up/tidy up the park **NB:** *ignore any mention of journey* • school visits/visits to school/going to school(s)	2
2.	(a)		lack/shortage of/don't get enough/not having an education	1
	(b)		• to recognise the (human) rights of girls • to address/solve/find a solution to the problems faced by girls/their problems • to increase the number/amount of girls who complete/get/have a (basic) education/schooling/school **(Any 2 from 3)**	2
	(c)		• do not complete secondary/high school (education) • illiterate **NB:** *blanks must be in the correct order*	2
	(d)		• the least/less well-paid/badly paid (jobs) • the least/less valued jobs/less value • domestic service/housekeeping/household chores/housework/house service/home service **(Any 2 from 3)**	2
	(e)		• study/go to school for 1 more year/a year longer/another year • a chance of/access to better jobs/employment/get better jobs • generate/earn/get <u>more</u> income/money for their families	3

Question			Expected Answer(s)	Max Mark
3.	(a)		• better/good/improved access to the Internet • communication technologies/technology to communicate/communicate through technology	2
	(b)	(i)	increases productivity/more productive/improves production **NB:** *ignore reference to employers/employees*	1
		(ii)	balance work (life) with family/personal (life)/work-life balance	1
	(c)		• she can be/stay in touch with/communicate with/contact her colleagues/workmates/co-workers (online) • <u>she can stay in touch/work/do this</u> from home/café/park **NB:** *any 2 places needed*	2
	(d)		• she gets up/gets out of bed early • she eats/has breakfast • she reads/checks/looks at emails • she puts on/wears/picks comfortable clothes • she walks/goes to the living room/lounge **(Any 3 from 5)**	3
	(e)		**BOTTOM BOX** – Working from home has many advantages **NB:** *if more than one box is ticked, 0 marks are awarded*	1

Writing

Please see the assessment criteria for Writing on pages 102–104.

Listening

Question			Expected Answer(s)	Max Mark
1.	(a)		• in the morning/every morning/ when she gets up • an hour and a half/1 hour 30 mins	2
	(b)		grandfather/grandpa/papa/granda	1
	(c)		romance/romantic/love (novels/ stories/books)	1
	(d)		• a little/a bit/quite/slightly boring • not realistic/unrealistic **(Any 1 from 2)**	1
	(e)		• to download apps/applications • to shop/buy/shopping (online)/ buying things/stuff/internet shopping	2
	(f)		**BOX 2** – she reads for enjoyment *NB: if more than one box is ticked, 0 marks are awarded*	1
2.	(a)		two years/summers ago	1
	(b)		four days	1
	(c)		(she can see) different artists/ groups/bands/musicians/singers on the same day/throughout the day/ on the one day	1
	(d)		• cinema/films/movies • theatre/plays • competitions/contests • dance/dancing • exhibitions/shows **(Any 2 from 5)**	2
	(e)		• to have a rest/to relax/chill out • to meet/to get to know people from all over the world/from other countries	2
	(f)	(i)	her parents don't like it/camping	1
		(ii)	• in her uncle's house/home/with her uncle/at her uncle's • in a house in the centre of the town/village • in a house in a nearby town/ village **(Any 1 from 3)**	1
	(g)		• she is older/old enough/grown up • they trust her • she is more independent/ independent enough **(Any 2 from 3)**	2
	(h)		**BOX 2** – enjoying the atmosphere *NB: if more than one box is ticked, 0 marks are awarded*	1

Acknowledgements

Permission has been sought from all relevant copyright holders and Hodder Gibson is grateful for the use of the following:

Image © jazzerup/Shutterstock.com (2014 Reading page 2);
Image © Featureflash/Shutterstock.com (2014 Reading page 4);
Image © Konstantin Chagin/Shutterstock.com (2014 Reading page 6);
Image © Stokkete/Shutterstock.com (2015 Reading page 2);
Image © zhu difeng/Shutterstock.com (2015 Reading page 4);
Image © Zurijeta/Shutterstock.com (2015 Reading page 6);
Image © Alexander Gordeyev/Shutterstock.com (2016 Reading page 2);
Image © De Visu/Shutterstock.com (2016 Reading page 4);
Image © fonzales/Shutterstock.com (2016 Reading page 6).